COLUMBIA

COMMON
ENGLISH USAGE
MISTAKES
AT SAT®

Richard Lee, Ph.D.

COLUMBIA PRESS

To Nancy S. T. , Philip, T. L., and Christina K. L

CONTENTS

INTRODUCTION

Columbia Common English Usage Mistakes at SAT is compiled to help you learn the absolutely essential grammar testing points and avoid the most common mistakes at SAT to raise your score! It has twenty lessons with each one having the following outstanding features:

- ERROR EXAMPLES: show you what kinds of mistakes most often made at SAT and how to correct them;
- GRAMMAR GUIDES: teach you the grammar rules absolutely essential to raise your SAT score;
- PRACTICE TESTS: Use sample Sentence Correction and Sentence Completion questions to test your grammar power and readiness for the real SAT;
- ANSWER KEYS: provide answers and explanations to help you avoid the mistakes forever to score higher on the SAT!

Columbia Common English Usage Mistakes at SAT is your grammar Bible! With the help of our fun and effective way to learn all the essential grammar testing points, you will be able to score higher on the SAT guaranteed!

CHAPTER ONE

INCORRECT

USE OF AN ARTICLE

LESSON 1

TESTING POINT: USE
ARTICLES CORRECTLY

ERROR EXAMPLE

WRONG: The scholarship that Philip received to study finance at Harvard University presented an unique opportunity.

RIGHT: The scholarship that Philip received to study finance at Harvard University presented <u>a</u> unique opportunity.

GRAMMAR GUIDE

In English, there are two kinds of articles: indefinite artices *a* and *an* and definite artice *the*.

For indefinite Articles, the basic difference between *a* and *an* is that *a* is used in front of consonants and *an* is used in front of vowels {a, e, i, o, u).

WRONG: It is an universal fact that we have only one earth.
RIGHT: It is a universal fact that we have only one earth.

The definite article *the* is used with singular and plural nouns or the nouns referring to things we already know about.

WRONG: Michael Blake is a player you can count on for success.

RIGHT: Michael Blake is the player you can count on for success.

PRACTICE TEST

Test 1. SENTENCE COMPLETION: Choose the CORRECT answer.

_____ responds to a wide range of frequencies.

   A. An human ear

   B..A human ear

Test 2. SENTENCE CORRECTION: Choose the INCORRECT word or phrase and CORRECT it.

1. We went to the store and bought new stove.

2. It is always difficult to make the decisions.

3. She doesn't have understanding of the subject yet.

4. Dogs make the good pets.

5. The honesty is a virtue.

ANSWER KEY

Test 1: B (use *an* only with words beginning with a vowel sound)

Test 2:

1. We went to the store and bought <u>a</u> new stove.

2. It is always difficult to <u>make decisions</u>.

3. She doesn't have <u>an</u> understanding of the subject yet.

4. Dogs make <u>good pets</u>.

5. <u>Honesty</u> is a virtue.

LESSON 2

TESTING POINT: CONFUSION OF ARTICLES: DISTINGUISH BETWEEN SPECIFIC AND GENERAL IDEAS

ERROR EXAMPLE

WRONG: Soil is composed of the mixture of organic matter called humus and inorganic matter derived from rocks.

RIGHT: Soil is composed of a mixture of organic matter called humus and inorganic matter derived from rocks.

GRAMMAR GUIDE

Both indefinite articles *a* and *an* and definite article *the* can be used before a singular countable noun. However, the definite article *the* refers to something specific or something we already know while indefinite articles *a* and *an* refer to something not specific or something we don't know exactly.

WRONG: Dr. Edward Johnson, the Dean of our college, is a person I want to see this afternoon.

RIGHT: Dr. Edward Johnson, the Dean of our college, is the person I want to see this afternoon.

WRONG: We went crab fishing on the chartered boat near Georgia Strait last Sunday.

RIGHT: We went crab fishing on a chartered boat near Georgia Strait last Sunday.

PRACTICE TEST

Test 1. SENTENCE COMPLETION: Choose the CORRECT answer.

A professor from Yale University will be giving_____at the Student Union building on Friday.

   A. a speech

   B. the speech

Test 2. SENTENCE CORRECTION: Choose the INCORRECT word or phrase and CORRECT it.

1. Alvin is a monitor of our English conversation class.

2. Seattle is considered only city in the North West that has the best climate.

3. My hometown is a place that has four clear seasons.

4. The university is where we can receive a more advanced education.

5. My grandpa's Snake Farm is a most exciting place I have ever been to in the world.

ANSWER KEY

Test 1: A (here we use indefinite article *a* because the speech is not being specifically known to us)

Test 2:

1. Alvin is <u>the</u> monitor of our English conversation class.

2. Seattle is considered <u>the</u> only city in the North West that has the best climate.

3. My hometown is <u>the</u> place that has four clear seasons.

4. <u>A</u> university is where we can receive a more advanced education.

5. My grandpa's Snake Farm is <u>the</u> most exciting place I have ever been to in the world.

CHAPTER TWO

INCORRECT

NUMBER OF A NOUN

LESSON 3

TESTING POINT: USE THE CORRECT SINGULAR OR PLURAL NOUN

ERROR EXAMPLE

WRONG: A U.S president can only serve a maximum of two

four-years terms.

RIGHT: A U.S president can only serve a maximum of two

four-year terms.

GRAMMAR GUIDE

One of the most common mistakes at English tests is that a singular noun is used where a plural noun is needed, or a plural noun is used where a singular noun is needed.

Remember that after these key words, *each, every, a, one,* and *single,* a singular noun is used.

Be careful that after these words, *many, several, both, various,* and *two,* plural nouns should be used.

WRONG: The auto shop has many parts for various type of expensive European cars.

RIGHT: The auto shop has many parts for various types of expensive European cars.

WRONG: On advices from his doctor, Michael Jones finally gave up smoking.

RIGHT: On advice from his doctor, Michael Jones finally gave up smoking.

PRACTICE TEST

Test 1. SENTENCE COMPLETION: Choose the CORRECT answer.

_____ were very upset after they had learned of the tuition increase next year.

   A. A number of student

   B. A number of students

Test 2. SENTENCE CORRECTION: Choose the INCORRECT word or phrase and CORRECT it.

1. Both of my friend are going to Australia to study this fall.

2. Each of the committee member voiced his opinion.

3. Every student should bear his responsibilities to be a good citizen.

4. One of the candidate wants to hold a public debate on campus safety.

5. A number of student activist have voted to establish a poverty fund for college students.

ANSWER KEY

Test 1: B (After *a number of*, always use plural noun.)

Test 2:

1. Both of my <u>friends</u> are going to Australia to study this fall.

2. Each of the committee <u>members</u> voiced his opinion.

3. Every student should bear his <u>responsibility</u> to be a good citizen.

4. One of the <u>candidates</u> wants to hold a public debate on campus safety.

5. A number of student <u>activists</u> have voted to establish a poverty

fund for college students. (here *student* is a noun used as an adjective modifying activists; therefore, it should be singular)

CHAPTER THREE

INCORRECT USE

OF A PRONOUN

LESSON 4

TESTING POINT: USE PERSONAL, POSSESSIVE, AND REFLEXIVE PRONOUNS CORRECTLY

ERROR EXAMPLE

WRONG: Everyone must sign their name at the reception desk.

RIGHT: Everyone must sign <u>his</u> name at the reception desk.

GRAMMAR GUIDE

Pronouns are used to replace or refer to nouns, gerunds, infinitives, and sometimes entire clauses. Pronouns change form depending on their functions in sentences.

Remember that always check personal, possessive, and reflexive pronouns for agreement.

WRONG: Nobody should be judged by their appearance.

RIGHT: Nobody should be judged by <u>his</u> appearance.

WRONG: We must let all citizens know his rights and obligations in
the society.

RIGHT: We must let all citizens know <u>their</u> rights and obligations in
the society.

PRACTICE TEST

Test 1. SENTENCE COMPLETION: Choose the CORRECT answer.

He is one of those people who always_____.

   A. brag about themselves

   B. brag about himself

Test 2. SENTENCE CORRECTION: Choose the INCORRECT word or phrase and CORRECT it.

1. Between you and I, the economic situation does not look bad.

2. It was him who knocked on the door last night.

3. Jack is as tall as me.

4. You don't have to worry about me. I can cook myself my dinner.

5. It is she, the one whom nobody likes.

ANSWER KEY

Test 1: A (Here you should use reflexive pronoun *themselves* because it refres to *people*.)

Test 2:

1. Between you and _me_, the economic situation does not look bad.

2. It was _he_ who knocked on the door last night.

3. Jack is as tall as _I_.

4. You don't have to worry about me. I can cook dinner _myself_.

5. It is _her_, the one whom nobody likes.

LESSON 5

TESTING POINT: USE REFLEXIVE PRONOUNS CORRECTLY

ERROR EXAMPLE

WRONG: According to the Fifth Amendment to the U.S. Constitution, nobody should be compelled to be a witness against themselves.

RIGHT: According to the Fifth Amendment to the U.S. Constitution, nobody should be compelled to be a witness against himself.

GRAMMAR GUIDE

In English, a reflexive pronoun (*myself, ourselves, yourself, yourselves, himself, herself, themselves, itself*) can be used as the complement of a sentence or a clause. It can also be used as the object of a preposition.

WRONG: When you take a test, you should always give you enough time to check the answers before you hand it in.

RIGHT: When you take a test, you should always give <u>yourself</u> enough time to check the answers before you hand it in.

WRONG: It seems everyone knows favouritism exists — but nobody wants to put his hand up and say he is guilty of it itself.

RIGHT: It seems everyone knows favouritism exists — but nobody wants to put his hand up and say he is guilty of it <u>himself</u>.

PRACTICE TEST

Test 1. SENTENCE COMPLETION: Choose the CORRECT answer.

All this would be apart from the failure of two generations of efforts to build a strong European framework_____.

   A. around Germany themselves.

   B. around Germany itself.

Test 2. SENTENCE CORRECTION: Choose the INCORRECT word or phrase and CORRECT it.

1. Be careful with these sharp tools or you will hurt to you.

2. A child can usually feed self by the age of six months.

3. Since nobody knew how to swim in my family, I had to teach me how to swim.

4. Help you to whatever you like, it is free.

5. A modern microwave that can clean it is really unbelievable.

ANSWER KEY

Test 1: B (here *Germany* is third person singular, therefore, *itself* should be used here.)

Test 2:

1. Be careful with these sharp tools or you will hurt <u>yourself</u>.

2. A child can usually feed <u>himself</u> by the age of six months.

3. Since nobody knew how to swim in my family, I had to teach <u>myslef</u> how to swim.

4. Help <u>yourself</u> to whatever you like, it is free.

5. A modern microwave that can clean <u>itself</u> is really unbelievable.

CHAPTER FOUR

INCORRECT

USE OF A VERB

LESSON 6

TESTING POINT: PROBLEMS

WITH PASSIVE VERBS

ERROR EXAMPLE

WRONG: The answer was knew by most of the students in our class.

RIGHT: The answer <u>was known</u> by most of the students in our class.

GRAMMAR GUIDE

Sentences in which the error is an incorrect passive or active are common in English tests. Therefore, you must be able to determine whether a passive verb (passive voice) rather than an active verb (active voice) is needed in a sentence and vice versa.

WRONG: Nobody should judge by his wallet.

RIGHT: Nobody <u>should be judged</u> by his wallet.

WRONG: A mystery is something that can't explain.

RIGHT: A mystery is something that <u>can't be explained.</u>

PRACTICE TEST

Test 1. SENTENCE COMPLETION: Choose the CORRECT answer.

Your laptop would not_____if you had not left it on the back seat of your car.

    A. have been stolen

    B. have stolen

Test 2. SENTENCE CORRECTION: Choose the INCORRECT word or phrase and CORRECT it.

1. Another man was being hired for the position yesterday.

2. A high-tech park is going to build near the university city.

3. I Have never been informed of his coming before he came.

4. All the building are been destroyed during the bombing.

5. We were gave a prize by the school district.

ANSWER KEY

Test 1: A (here passive voice *have been stolen* must be used)

Test 2:

1. Another man <u>was hired</u> for the position yesterday.

2. A high-tech park is going <u>to be built</u> near the university city.

3. I <u>had never been informed</u> of his coming before he came.

4. All the buildings <u>were destroyed</u> during the bombing.

5. We <u>were given</u> a prize by the school district.

LESSON 7

TESTING POINT: USE *HAVE* +

PAST PARTICIPLE AND *HAD* + PAST

PARTICIPLE CORRECTLY

ERROR EXAMPLE

WRONG: If I had had a million dollars, I would build a private
language school then.

RIGHT: If I had had a million dollars, I <u>would have built</u> a private
language school then.

GRAMMAR GUIDE

The Present Perfect Tense (*have* + past participle) and the Past Perfect

Tense (*had* + past participle) have completely different uses.

The present perfect refers to something happened in the past and continued to present. At the time of speaking, the action is completed.

WRONG: William Black lived in Vancouver for almost twenty years.

RIGHT: William Black has lived in Vancouver for almost twenty years.

WRONG: At the start of the twenty-first century, cell phones have become very popular among teenagers.

RIGHT: At the start of the twenty-first century, cell phones became very popular among teenagers.

The past perfect refers to something that had been completed before something happened in the past.

WRONG: Jennifer has finished her dinner when Jack came to pick her up.

RIGHT: Jennifer had finished her dinner when Jack came to pick her up.

WRONG: Mary already went to sleep when we arrived.

RIGHT: Mary had already gone to sleep when we arrived.

PRACTICE TEST

Test 1. SENTENCE COMPLETION: Choose the CORRECT answer.

Had I known you at Harvard Business School, we_____.

    A. would come business partners

    B. would have become business partners

Test 2. SENTENCE CORRECTION: Choose the INCORRECT word or phrase and CORRECT it.

1. After I complete my studies in America, I will return to my own country.

2. When she began her schooling, she has already memorized 3000 new words.

3. Since I am grown up now, I should help my parents in finances.

4. Up to now, the city had built five community centres.

5. By the end of 1988, the number of students in the country risen to 12 million.

ANSWER KEY

Test 1: B (here in the adverbial clause of past conditional, it is the past perfect tense, therefore, in the main clause, it should be past future perfect tense: *would have become*)

Test 2:

1. After I have completed my studies in America, I will return to my own country.

2. When she began her schooling, she had already memorized 3000 new words.

3. Since I have grown up now, I should help my parents in finances.

4. Up to now, the city has built five community centres.

5. By the end of 1988, the number of students in the country had risen to 12 million.

LESSON 8

TESTING POINT:

EMPHASIS: NOUNS DERIVED

FROM SUBJUNCTIVE VERBS

ERROR EXAMPLE

WRONG: The proposal that our downtown college bookstore stays open on Sundays was welcomed.

RIGHT: The proposal that our downtown college bookstore stay open on Sundays was welcomed.

GRAMMAR GUIDE

Remember that the following nouns derived from subjunctive verbs are most often used in this pattern:

demand, insistenc, preference, proposal, recommendation, request requirement, suggestion:

WRONG: The recommendation that school teachers should be
evaluated for stipend every year was approved.

RIGHT: The recommendation that school teachers <u>be evaluated</u> for
stipend every year was approved.

PRACTICE TEST

Test 1. SENTENCE COMPLETION: Choose the CORRECT answer.

Everybody liked my suggestion that Gordon McDonald _____.

   A. is running for the next President of the United States

   B. run for the next President of the United States

Test 2. SENTENCE CORRECTION: Choose the INCORRECT word or phrase and CORRECT it.

1. He complied with the requirement that all graduate students in education should write a thesis.

2. The committee refused the request that the prerequisite shall be waived.

3. She ignored the suggestion that she gets more exercise.

4. The terrorist's demand that the airline provides a plane will not be met by the deadline.

5. He regretted not having followed his advisor's recommendation that he dropping the class.

ANSWER KEY

Test 1: B (here the simple form of the verb *run* must be used even if it is in the third person singular)

Test 2:

1. He complied with the requirement that all graduate students in education <u>write</u> a thesis.

2. The committee refused the request that the prerequisite <u>be waived</u>.

3. She ignored the suggestion that she <u>get </u>more exercise.

4. The terrorist's demand that the airline<u> provide</u> a plane will not be met by the deadline.

5. He regretted not having followed his advisor's recommendation that he <u>drop</u> the class.

LESSON 9

TESTING POINT: INVERT

THE SUBJECT AND VERB

WITH CONDITIONALS

ERROR EXAMPLE

WRONG: Had you studied harder, your test score should be higher.

RIGHT: Had you studied harder, your test score would have been higher.

GRAMMAR GUIDE

The inversion of the subject and verb in conditional structures occurs when the helping verb in the conditional clause is *had, should,* or *were,* and the conditional connector *if* is omitted.

WRONG: I would definitely help you was I in a position to help.

RIGHT: I would definitely help you <u>were</u> I in a position to help.

PRACTICE TEST

Test 1. SENTENCE COMPLETION: Choose the CORRECT answer.

Had it not been for your invaluable assistance with my application, _____.

   A.I would not have been accepted by Harvard Law School

   B. I would not be accepted by Harvard Law School

Test 2. SENTENCE CORRECTION: Choose the INCORRECT word or phrase and CORRECT it.

1. Was she there, she would make a speech at the university.

2. Has there been a chance, I would have taken it.

3. Lost your job, what would you have done?

4. Had they asked me, I would give my opinion yesterday.

5. Had Bob study more, he would have passed the test.

ANSWER KEY

Test 1: A (In the conditional clause, we used past perfect tense, therefore, in the main clause, we should use past future perfect tense: *would not have been accepted.*)

Test 2:

1. Were she there, she would make a speech at the university.

2. Had there been a chance, I would have taken it.

3. Had you lost your job, what would you have done?

4. Had they asked me, I would have given my opinion yesterday.

5. Had Bob studied more, he would have passed the test.

LESSON 10

TESTING POINT:

ERRORS WITH VERBALS

ERROR EXAMPLE

WRONG: The exhausting basketball players were too tired to move after they had won the championship.

RIGHT: The exhausted basketball players were too tired to move after they had won the championship.

GRAMMAR GUIDE

Verbals are participles, gerunds, and infinitives. They can be used as adjectives.

For present participles, they end with *–ing*; for past participles, they end with *–ed*.

When modifying nouns, present participles tend to have active meaning whereas past participles have passive meaning.

WRONG: The millionaire's stealing Land Rover was finally

recovered with the help of the police.

RIGHT: The millionaire's <u>stolen</u> Land Rover was finally recovered

with the help of the police.

Gerunds are verbal nouns. They end in *–ing* like the present participle. They can be used as the subjects of verbs, the objects of prepositions and certain verbs.

WRONG: Young people should always look forward to see miracles

happen in their lives.

RIGHT: Young people should always look forward to <u>seeing</u>

miracles happen in their lives.

Infinitives are formed with *to* plus the simple form of the verb.

They can be used as the subjects of verbs and the objects of certain

verbs.

WRONG: John Glenn was the first American orbiting the Earth.

RIGHT: John Glenn was the first American <u>to orbit</u> the Earth.

PRACTICE TEST

Test 1. SENTENCE COMPLETION: Choose the CORRECT answer.

Tenants of this building are advised to shut the windows in winter; for we_____.

    A. can not afford heating the outside

    B. can not afford to heat the outside

Test 2. SENTENCE CORRECTION: Choose the INCORRECT word or phrase and CORRECT it.

1. This new sports car is very easy driving.

2. The most important discovery knowing to all might be DNA.

3. No rich person can afford feeding such a hungry nation after the war.

4. Have finished dinner, we took a walk along the Thames.

5. No one looks forward to hear bad news after the college entrance exam.

ANSWER KEY

Test 1: B (here after *afford*, an infinitive *to heat* must be used instead of a gerund)

Test 2:

1. This new sports car is very easy to drive.

2. The most important discovery known to all might be DNA.

3. No rich person can afford *to* feed such a hungry nation after the war.

4. Having finished dinner, we took a walk along the Thames.

5. No one looks forward to hearing bad news after the college entrance exam.

LESSON 11

TESTING POINT:

PROBLEMS WITH INFINITIVES

ERROR EXAMPLE

WRONG: The first man landing on the moon was Neil Armstrong.

RIGHT: The first man <u>to land</u> on the moon was Neil Armstrong.

GRAMMAR GUIDE

Infinitives are formed with *to* plus the simple form of the verb.

They can be used as the subjects of verbs and the objects of certain

verbs.

WRONG: Johny got lost in New York City because he forgot reading the direction on the tourist map.

RIGHT: Johny got lost in New York City because he forgot

to read the direction on the tourist map.

Infinitives can be used as adjective phrases after noun phrases.

WRONG: Jack Daniel was the only man receiving this privilege

RIGHT: Jack Daniel was the only man to receive this privilege.

Infinitives can also be used to show purpose.

WRONG: He is learning Chinese for finding a job in China.

RIGHT: He is learning Chinese to find a job in China.

PRACTICE TEST

Test 1. SENTENCE COMPLETION: Choose the CORRECT answer.

_____on the college entrance test, we must study hard and be fully prepared.

A. To get a higher score

B. Getting a higher score

Test 2. SENTENCE CORRECTION: Choose the INCORRECT word or phrase and CORRECT it.

1. She is reputed to be a spy for KGB during the Cold War.

2. The injured worker was reported to die the day before.

3. They chose to not have attended the meeting.

4. Our job is help you to pass the standardized exam.

5. The police officer offered give her a ride home because she was drunk.

ANSWER KEY

Test 1: A (here an infinitive *to get*... must be used as the adverbial of purpose)

Test 2:

1. She is reputed to have been a spy for the KGB during the Cold War.

2. The injured worker was reported to have died the day before.

3. They chose not to attend the meeting.

4. Our job is to help you to pass the standardized exam.

5. The police officer offered to give her a ride home because she was drunk.

CHAPTER FIVE

ADVERB/ADJECTIVE CONFUSION

LESSON **12**

TESTING POINT: USE BASIC ADJECTIVES AND ADVERBS CORRECTLY

ERROR EXAMPLE

WRONG: The newly released Hollywood movie tells an extreme moving story.

RIGHT: The newly released Hollywood movie tells an <u>extremely</u> moving story.

GRAMMAR GUIDE

In English, adjectives and advrbs have different functions in a

sentence. Basically, an adjective is used to modify a noun or a pronoun.

WRONG: Modern art is on display at the Guggenhein Museum, a building with an unusually design.

RIGHT: Modern art is on display at the Guggenhein Museum, a building with an <u>unusual</u> design.

An adverb is used to modify a verb, an adjective or another

adverb.

WRONG: Our offshore telephone call centres were successful established in 2005.

RIGHT: Our offshore telephone call centres were <u>successfully</u> established in 2005.

WRONG: I worked real hard on Microeconomics, but failed.

RIGHT: I worked <u>really hard</u> on Microeconomics, but failed.

PRACTICE TEST

Test 1. SENTENCE COMPLETION: Choose the CORRECT answer.

Mary Lopez got almost full marks on her biology final because she _____ for it.

A. had studied very hardly

B. had studied very hard

Test 2. SENTENCE CORRECTION: Choose the INCORRECT word or phrase and CORRECT it.

1. Jake was extreme happy to see her coming back from vacation in Africa.
2. The deadly silence of the night even scared bravest soldiers.
3. You must do it very carefully, if not perfect.
4. He worked very hardly on his college entrance exams.
5. You should order that book real soon.

ANSWER KEY

Test 1: B (Here *hard* must be used because *hardly* means *almost not*)

Test 2:

1. Jake was extremely happy to see her coming back from vacation in Africa.

2. The dead silence of the night even scared the bravest soldiers.

3. You must do it very carefully, if not perfectly.

4. He worked very hard on his college entrance exams.

5. You should order that book <u>really</u> soon.

CHAPTER SIX

INCORRECT USE

OF A PREPOSITON

LESSON 13

TESTING POINT: RECOGNIZE INCORRECT PREPOSITIONS AND PREPOSITIONAL PHRASES

ERROR EXAMPLE

WRONG: I know that I can always rely in you when I am in trouble at school.

RIGHT: I know that I can always rely on you when I am in trouble at school.

GRAMMAR GUIDE

In English, single prepositions are easy to master, however,

prepositional phrases are very hard to handle. A prepositional phrase consists of a preposition and an object.

WRONG: The young artist earns her living of painting pictures for tourists in the park.

RIGHT: The young artist earns her living <u>by painting pictures</u> for tourists in the park.

WRONG: You can always learn what mistakes you have made in your practice exercise to do better in the real exam.

RIGHT: You can always learn <u>from what mistakes you have made</u> in your practice exercise to do better in the real exam.

PRACTICE TEST

Test 1. SENTENCE COMPLETION: Choose the CORRECT answer.

Russell MacDonald finally_____me about setting up a branch office in Asia.

   A. agreed to

   B. agreed with

Test 2. SENTENCE CORRECTION: Choose the INCORRECT word or phrase and CORRECT it.

1. I look forward for seeing you at the registration time.

2. Thomas has always been interested to sing at KTV.

3. We are very sorry to keep you here waiting..

4. He is very disappointed about his test score on the exam.

5. During the summer I usually work at my grandpa's snake farm.

ANSWER KEY

Test 1: B (*Agree with* is usually used with *somebody*. *Agree to* is usually followed by *something*.)

Test 2:

1. I look forward to seeing you at the registration time.

2. Thomas has always been interested in singing at KTV.

3. We are very sorry for keeping you here waiting.

4. He is very disappointed at his test score on the exam.

5. During the summer I usually work on my grandpa's snake farm.

LESSON 14

TESTING POINT: ERRORS

WITH PREPOSITIONS

ERROR EXAMPLE

WRONG: He always looks up to those who are senior to him in rank, and looks down at those who are junior to him in rank.

RIGHT: He always looks up to those who are senior to him in rank, and <u>looks down upon</u> those who are junior to him in rank.

GRAMMAR GUIDE

Remember that being able to use prepositions correctly will definitely help you score a few points higher on the test, therefore, you should always try to memorize the use of the most frequently tested prepositions. The following are some typical examples:

Between and *among*: *between* is used with two nouns, or persons or things, *among* is used among three nouns or persons or things.

WRONG: John Obama is the tallest between the boys in my class.

RIGHT: John Obama is the tallest <u>among</u> the boys in my class.

But and *except:* they have the same kind of use, however never confuse *except* with *excepting* or *exception.*

WRONG: No one excepting Cathy knows much about our secret.

RIGHT: No one <u>but</u> Cathy knows much about our secret.

Instead of and *Instead:* remember that never confuse *instead of* with *instead. Instead of* is a phrasal preposition whereas *instead* is an adverb.

WRONG: But more than half revealed that they intended to send an

electronic greeting card, instead a traditional one

RIGHT: But more than half revealed that they intended to send an

electronic greeting card, <u>instead of</u> a traditional one.

PRACTICE TEST

Test 1. SENTENCE COMPLETION: Choose the CORRECT answer.

To lead a well-balanced life, you need_____.

    A. to have other interests beside studying

    B. to have other interests besides studying

Test 2. SENTENCE CORRECTION: Choose the INCORRECT word or phrase and CORRECT it.

1. The next performance begins in dusk.

2. These toys are made with the Indians living in Northern Alberta.

3. Joyce is quite satisfied by his new apartment downtown.

4. The students are bored for sitting all day in the classroom.

5. What time do you think you will arrive to Boston?

ANSWER KEY

Test 1: B (*besides* means *in addition to,* never confuse *besides* with *beside*)

Test 2:

1. The next performance begins at dusk.

2. These toys are made by the Indians living in Northern Alberta.

3. Joyce is quite satisfied with his new apartment downtown.

4. The students are bored with sitting all day in the classroom.

5. What time do you think you will arrive in Boston?

CHAPTER SEVEN

FAULTY DICTION

LESSON 15

TESTING POINT: USE *BORROW* AND *LEND, LET* AND *LEAVE* CORRECTLY

ERROR EXAMPLE

WRONG: Small companies can lend money from the banks to either expand or consolidate their business.

RIGHT: Small companies can borrow money from the banks to either expand or consolidate their business.

GRAMMAR GUIDE

The words *borrow* and *lend* seem to be similar, but completely different in meaning. To *borrow* means to take something from somebody and give it back, but to *lend* is to give something to somebody and take it back.

WRONG: The crops are dying out because there is a little rain this
summer.

RIGHT: The crops are dying out because there is little rain this
summer.

As for *a few* and *few, a few* means some, whereas *few* means

almost not any. Both of them modify countable nouns.

WRONG: Pamela feels very lonely on the weekend; for she has a few
friends in Los Angeles.

RIGHT: Pamela feels very lonely on the weekend; for she has

few friends in Los Angeles.

To let and to *leave* sound similar, but similar in meaning. *To let* means

to allow or to permit.

WRONG: Our English teacher allows us speak no other language but
English both in class and at home.

RIGHT: Our English teacher <u>lets</u> us speak no other language but English both in class and at home.

To leave means to let someone or something remain, and it also means *to go* or *to depart.*

WRONG: Joyce let her cell phone on the airplane yesterday.

RIGHT: Joyce <u>left</u> her cell phone on the airplane yesterday.

PRACTICE TEST

Test 1. SENTENCE COMPLETION: Choose the CORRECT answer.

Before you leave for Paris, please_____if you need anything.

   A. let me to know

   B. let me know

Test 2. SENTENCE CORRECTION: Choose the INCORRECT word or phrase and CORRECT it.

1. Stan had an accident while he was driving the car that his cousin had borrowed him.

2. Would you please borrow me your pen?

3. Can I lend this dictionary for a few minutes while I check my composition?

4. Although her doctor allowed her family to visit her, he wouldn't leave anyone else go into her room.

5. You can let your car in long-term parking until you come back.

ANSWER KEY

Test 1: B (*let* somebody *do* something, never put *to* in front of the simple verb)

Test 2:

1. Stan had an accident while he was driving the car that his cousin <u>had lent</u> him.

2. Would you please <u>lend</u> me your pen?

3. Can I <u>borrow</u> this dictionary for a few minutes while I check my composition?

4. Although her doctor allowed her family to visit her, he wouldn't <u>let</u> anyone else go into her room.

5. You can <u>leave</u> your car in long-term parking until you come back.

LESSON 16

TESTING POINT: USE *A LITTLE* AND *LITTLE*, *A FEW* AND *FEW* CORRECTLY

ERROR EXAMPLE

WRONG: Few information is currently available as to whether the governor will resign after the bribery scandal.

RIGHT: Little information is currently available as to whether the governor will resign after the bribery scandal.

GRAMMAR GUIDE

The difference between *a little* and *little* is that *a little* means some;

whereas *little* means *almost not any*. Both of them modify uncountable nouns.

WRONG: The crops are dying out because there is a little rain this

summer.

RIGHT: The crops are dying out because there is <u>little</u> rain this

summer.

As for *a few* and *few, a few* means some, whereas *few* means

almost not any. Both of them modify countable nouns.

WRONG: Pamela feels very lonely on the weekend; for she has a few

friends in Los Angeles.

RIGHT: Pamela feels very lonely on the weekend; for she has

<u>few</u> friends in Los Angeles.

PRACTICE TEST

Test 1. SENTENCE COMPLETION: Choose the CORRECT answer.

I am sure I will get a very high score this time because I made_____ on the exam.

A. only a little mistakes

B. only a few mistakes

Test 2. SENTENCE CORRECTION: Choose the INCORRECT word or phrase and CORRECT it.

1. Give me little butter, please.

2. We have a little news about the plane crash.

3. There are few tickets left for the concert.

4. A few people in my apartment building are friendly.

5. She speaks a little French.

ANSWER KEY

Test 1: B (here *mistake* is a countable noun, therefore, *a few* should be used.)

Test 2:

1. Give me a little butter, please.

2. We have little news about the plane crash.

3. There are a few tickets left for the concert.

4. Few people in my apartment building are friendly.

5. She speaks little French.

CHAPTER EIGHT

NON-STANDARD WORDS, EXPRESSIONS, OR IDIOMS

LESSON 17

TESTING POINT: CHECK WORD FORM: WORDS THAT DON'T EXIST IN ENGLISH

ERROR EXAMPLE

WRONG: The defectator sought refuge at the U.S. Embassy in Paris.

RIGHT: The <u>defector</u> sought refuge at the U.S. Embassy in Paris.

GRAMMAR GUIDE

In English tests,, a word that does not exist in English is sometimes used to confuse you. However, these non-standard words are closely related to real English word forms. The following are a few of the most common examples:

WRONG: George Vancouver may not have been the first explorator who have discovered Vancouver.

RIGHT: George Vancouver may not have been the first <u>explorer</u> who have discovered Vancouver.

WRONG: The current estable situation is very good for the economy.

RIGHT: The current <u>stable</u> situation is very good for the economy.

WRONG: When we travel abroad, we need to bring a universal adaptator for our laptops and cell phones.

RIGHT: When we travel abroad, we need to bring a universal <u>adaptor</u> for our laptops and cell phones.

PRACTICE TEST

Test 1. SENTENCE COMPLETION: Choose the CORRECT answer.

It is very easy to recycle plastic, just take it to your local _____.

   A. plastic collection point

   B. plastical collection point

Test 2. SENTENCE CORRECTION: Choose the INCORRECT word or phrase and CORRECT it.

1. The commandor ordered the soldiers to march on.

2. We should give our consentment to the proposal.

3. The economer predicted the crash of the stock market.

4. What you have just said is absolutely ture.

5. The political commentater is optimistic about the presidential election.

ANSWER KEY

Test 1: A (Here you must use *plastic* instead of *plastical* because there is no such word as *plastical* in English.)

Test 2:

1. The <u>commander</u> ordered the soldiers to march on.

2. We should give our <u>consent</u> to the proposal.

3. The <u>economist</u> predicted the crash of the stock market.

4. What you have just said is absolutely <u>true</u>.

5. The political <u>commentator</u> is optimistic about the presidential election.

CHAPTER NINE

INCORRECT DEGREE

OF COMPARISON

LESSON 18

TESTING POINT: CHECK EQUATIVE, COMPARATIVE, AND SUPERLATIVE DEGREE

ERROR EXAMPLE

WRONG: Vancouver is more beautiful than any city in the world.

RIGHT: Vancouver is more beautiful than <u>any other</u> city in the world.

.

GRAMMAR GUIDE

There are three kinds of comparison in English. They are the equative, comparative, and the superlative.

Equative degree is used to show equality.

WRONG: This building is as tall like that one by the seaside.

RIGHT: This building is <u>as</u> tall <u>as</u> that one by the seaside.

The comparative degree is used to compare two things that are not equal. In your test, when you see the word *more*, look for *than*.

WRONG: Michael is definitely more smarter than Jack Daniels.

RIGHT: Michael is definitely smarter than Jack Daniels.

The superlative degree is used to compare three or more things that are not equal. When you see the words like *one of the*, look for *most* or a word ending in *–est*.

WRONG: One of the most exciting thing for parents is a baby's first word spoken like a miracle..

RIGHT: <u>One of</u> the most exciting <u>things</u> for parents is a baby's first word spoken like a miracle.

PRACTICE TEST

Test 1. SENTENCE COMPLETION: Choose the CORRECT answer.

He is the _____ person in the class to be late.

A. least possible

B. less possible

Test 2. SENTENCE CORRECTION: Choose the INCORRECT word or phrase and CORRECT it.

1. Our building is the same height like yours.

2. Jennifer is definitely smart as Marilyn.

3. The population of my hometown is much smaller than Shanghai.

4. The higher the degree you have, the more high wage you will get.

5. One of the most difficult problem in math is logical reasoning.

ANSWER KEY

Test 1: A (Here you should use *least* because there must be at least three or more students in a class.)

Test 2:

1. Our building is <u>the same</u> height *as* yours.

2. Jennifer is definitely <u>as</u> smart <u>as</u> Marilyn.

3. The population of my hometown is much smaller than <u>that of</u> Shanghai.

4. The higher the degree you have, the <u>higher</u> the wage you will get.

5. One of the most difficult <u>problems</u> in math is logical reasoning.

LESSON 19

TESTING POINT:

COMPARATIVE ESTIMATES:

-*MORE THAN* AND *LESS THAN*

ERROR EXAMPLE

WRONG: He said that the company had more than a hundred employee, but he declined to comment further.

RIGHT: He said that the company had more than a hundred employees, but he declined to comment further.

GRAMMAR GUIDE

More than or *less than* is used before a specific number to express an estimate that may be a little more or a little less than the number.

WRONG: Nancy has more than twenty apartments downtown, but she has few than ten thousand dollars in her bank account.

RIGHT: Nancy has more than twenty apartments downtown, but she has less than ten thousand dollars in her bank account.

PRACTICE TEST

Test 1. SENTENCE COMPLETION: Choose the CORRECT answer.

In the Longwood Garden, you can see_____a thousand kinds of flowers and exotic plants.

A. more than

B. many

Test 2. SENTENCE CORRECTION: Choose the INCORRECT word or phrase and CORRECT it.

1. More one hundred people came to the meeting.

2. We have lived in the United States for as less than seven years.

3. The main library has more as one million volumes.

4. A new shopping center on the north side will have five hundred shops more than.

5. There are most than fifty students in the lab, but only two computers.

ANSWER KEY

Test 1: A (here more than should be used because we have a specific number *a thousand kinds*)

Test 2:

1. <u>More than one hundred</u> people came to the meeting.

2. We have lived in the United States for <u>less than seven years</u>.

3. The main library has <u>more than one million</u> volumes.

4. A new shopping center on the north side will have <u>more than five hundred</u> shops.

5. There are <u>more than fifty</u> students in the lab, but only two computers.

CHAPTER TEN

CONFUSION BETWEEN WORDS WITH SIMILAR SOUNDS (HOMOPHONES OR NEAR-HOMOPHONES)

LESSON 20

TESTING POINT:

USE WORDS WITH SIMILAR

SOUNDS CORRECTLY

ERROR EXAMPLE

WRONG: Sharon's remark of someone excepting bribery really annoyed her boss.

RIGHT: Sharon's remark of someone <u>accepting</u> bribery really annoyed her boss.

GRAMMAR GUIDE

In English, words with similar sounds are called homophones or homonyms. They look alike or sound alike (or both) but have very different meanings. The following are the most common homophones you should try to remember:

accept/except

advice/advise

allusion/illusion

by/buy/bye

capital/capitol

complement/compliment

council/counsel

discreet/discrete

dual/duel

elicit/illicit

eminent/imminent

fair/fare

lie/lye

meat/meat/mete

role/roll

scene/seen

stationary/stationery

whine/wine

WRONG: Dr. Johnson is one of the most imminent scholars on Romanticism in this century.

RIGHT: Dr. Johnson is one of the most <u>eminent</u> scholars on Romanticism in this century.

PRACTICE TEST

Test 1. SENTENCE COMPLETION: Choose the CORRECT answer.

"Women cannot and_____," she said, before telling a fraudulent tale of shopping and false price tags.

    A. do not lye

    B. do not lie

Test 2. SENTENCE CORRECTION: Choose the INCORRECT word or phrase and CORRECT it.

1. She was too discrete to mention the money in front of her mother.

2. The police illicited the truth from her family.

3. Without stationary we would not be able to do our job at all.

4. We don't have enough capitol to expand to Asia now.

5. A survey by The Sleep Counsel showed a quarter of men never wake up in a bad mood, compared to just one in seven women

ANSWER KEY

Test 1: B (*Lye* and *lie* have totally different meanings: *lye* is a strong alkaline substance whereas *lie* means telling something that is not true.)

Test 2:

1. She was too <u>discreet</u> to mention the money in front of her mother.

2. The police <u>elicited</u> the truth from her family.

3. Without <u>stationery</u> we would not be able to do our job at all.

4. We don't have enough <u>capital</u> to expand to Asia now.

5. A survey by The Sleep <u>Council</u> showed a quarter of men never wake up in a bad mood, compared to just one in seven women

ACKNOWLEDGEMENTS

The author would like to thank his colleagues and students for bring some of these mistakes to life.

The author and publisher are grateful to those who have made this publication possible by providing all kinds of support from editing, graphic design, and proof-reading. Efforts have been made to identify the source of materials used in this book, however, it has not always been possible to identify the sources of all the materials used, or to trace the copyright holders. If any omissions are brought to our attention, we will be happy to include the appropriate aknowlegements on reprinting.

ABOUT THE AUTHOR

Dr. Richard Lee is a professor of English and distinguished publishing scholar with more than ten books published under his name. His books are available on Amazon, other online stores, and in bookstores worldwide. Dr, Lee pursued his graduate education at the University of Rochester and the University of British Columbia and got his Ph.D. in English. Dr. Lee lives in beautiful Vancouver, British Columbia.

www.ingramcontent.com/pod-product-compliance
Lightning Source LLC
Chambersburg PA
CBHW071622040426
42452CB00009B/1444